CEDAR MILL COMM LIBRARY
12505 NW CORNELL RD
PORTLAND, OR 97229
(503) 644-0043
WITHDRAWN
CEDAR MILL LIBRARY

MICHELLE
OBAMA

MICHELLE OBAMA

Speeches on Life, Love, and American Values

Edited by Stacie Vander Pol

pacps
Pacific Publishing Studio

Copyright © 2009 by Pacific Publishing Studio
All rights reserved.

Published in the United States by Beacon Hill, an imprint of Pacific
Publishing Studio.
www.PacPS.com

ISBN -978-0-9823756-3-1

To order a copy of this book, visit www.Amazon.com.
No part of this book may be reproduced in any form unless written
permission is granted from the author or publisher. No electronic
reproductions, information storage, or retrieval systems may be used or
applied to any part of this book without written permission. Pacific
Publishing Studio books are available at discounts for bulk purchases in the
United States by institution, corporations, and other groups and
organizations. For information on bulk purchases, contact Pacific Publishing
Studio through the website at www.PacPS.com.

Special acknowledgement is made to the following:
Introduction: Stacie Vander Pol
Front Cover Photography: www.army.mil
Back Cover Photography: Richard Pross
Michelle Obama Bio: www.whitehouse.gov
Transcription: Pacific Publishing Studio

Table of Contents

Part 2

Speeches Given during the Presidential Race

Appendix

Introduction

In January of 2009, Michelle Obama made history when she became the first ever African-American First Lady of the United States. By working on the campaign trail to share his vision, she played an integral role in the election of her husband, Barack Obama. In the process, Americans came to know, respect, and admire the woman who was soon to become their next First Lady.

Through speeches, interviews, and town hall meetings, Michelle Obama inspired women and men all over the world and continues to serve as an impressive role model. Through her success as a professional, a mother, and a wife, Michelle Obama emulates what is possible for all women, no matter their race, class, or family background.

Michelle Obama asks of us to be better citizens and to serve the world as we serve ourselves. She empathizes with our struggles and fears, and understands our journey through this world as a mother, a friend, a daughter, and a wife.

She has been called a fashion icon and compared to Jacqueline Kennedy for her style and grace. She has been likened to Princess Diana for her passion and desire to champion causes for the less fortunate. She embodies the American story—the American Dream.

This book is a collection of public speeches Michelle Obama gave while campaigning for her husband over a period of twenty months during the 2008 presidential campaign. In it, she speaks to small communities, women's groups, military spouses, students, and local communities as well as the entire nation. She shares her view of the world, her faith in her husband, her commitment to her children, and her belief in the strength of the human spirit.

On January 25, at the Democratic National Convention, Michelle Obama addressed a live audience of 20,000 people while over 22 million viewers watched on television. That speech, along with many others is included in here. Let them serve as inspiration and as a permanent record of our nation's history.

MICHELLE OBAMA Bio

White House First Lady

Born 1964

When people ask Michelle Obama to describe herself, she doesn't hesitate. First and foremost, she is Malia and Sasha's mom.

But before she was a mother—or a wife, lawyer, or public servant—she was Fraser and Marian Robinson's daughter.

The Robinsons lived in a brick bungalow on the South Side of Chicago. Fraser was a pump operator for the Chicago Water Department, and despite being diagnosed with multiple sclerosis at a young age, he rarely missed a day of work. Marian stayed home to raise Michelle and her brother, Craig—skillfully managing a busy household filled with love, laughter, and important life lessons.

A product of Chicago public schools, Michelle studied sociology and African-American studies at Princeton University. After graduating from Harvard Law School in 1988, she joined the Chicago law firm Sidley & Austin, where she later met the man who would become the love of her life.

After a few years, Michelle decided her true calling lay in encouraging people to serve their communities and their neighbors. She served as assistant commissioner of planning and development in Chicago's City Hall before becoming the founding executive director of the Chicago chapter of Public Allies, an AmeriCorps program that prepares youth for public service.

In 1996, Michelle joined the University of Chicago with a vision of bringing campus and community together. As associate dean of student services, she developed the university's first community service program, and under her leadership as vice president of community and external affairs for the University of Chicago Medical Center, volunteerism skyrocketed.

As First Lady, Michelle Obama looks forward to continuing her work on the issues close to her heart: supporting military families, helping working women balance career and family, and encouraging national service.

Michelle and Barack Obama have two daughters: Malia and Sasha. Like their mother, the girls were born on the South Side of Chicago.[1]

---

[1] Retrieved from the public records at whitehouse.gov.

Section 1

This section includes speeches given by Michelle Obama during sixteen months of the primary race: April of 2007 through July of 2008. Speeches are in sequential order.

Meeting Barack

Their Story

Michelle reflects on her first impressions of Barack and the life they now share together.

"The first time I met Barack was at our law firm. I was a first year associate. He was funny; he was very self-deprecating. He had this amazing background and story. Barack had always talked about how he went to law school, not to cash out, but to try to make change. And he thought that the education he would acquire would give him the tools to come back and do more. He told me that he was a community organizer, and I didn't quite know what community organizing was. I'd never met anybody who was a community organizer.

In the world of corporate America that I was in, I certainly didn't find many young people who were that engaged in the community. He invited me to go with him to a training that he was doing on the far South Side in a small church.

So we walk in and he takes off his suit jacket. He loosens his tie, rolls up his sleeves, and he launches into what I think was the most eloquent discussion about 'the world as it is' and 'the world as it should be.' And how the work of community organizing is there to make the two less separate. And he connected with every single person in that room. There were a lot of Amens going on. So I thought, this guy is pretty special.

I am the youngest of two children and grew up in modest conditions. My father was a city worker. My mom was a stay at home mother.

Barack was raised in a teeny little apartment in Honolulu. I grew up in a teeny little apartment on the South Side of Chicago. And what drives Barack are these shared values which I call, 'good ole Midwestern values.'

We believe in hard work. We believe that you speak what's on your mind. Your word is your bond. You treat people with respect and dignity.

Our girls, Malia and Sasha, are the light of our lives. They keep us grounded and whole because they're kids. They are eight and five. And they care about getting a dog, and what they've done today, and how their lives are interesting and full. And what we are reminded of every day when we see them is that every child should be able to enjoy what they enjoy: that freedom of just having so much opportunity. Too many children in our country don't have that and it's not enough that our girls do.

It's very difficult to live this cozy and content life knowing that you possibly had a chance to do more for more people. And that's what we hope we can do."

Manchester, New Hampshire

A campaign event

April 4, 2007

Michelle introduces herself to New Hampshire voters and speaks about her own personal upbringing and about how family has influenced her life.

"This journey that we've been on is just still amazing to me. I am still overwhelmed by it. In fact, I tease Barack all the time when we go to places and somebody says, 'there's a thousand people in there to see you,' and I think well *who* are they there to see? Is it Bruce Springsteen or somebody else? Because I'm still trying to reconcile these two images of Barack Obama: there's Barack Obama the phenomenon and then there's the guy who lives at my house.

And that guy's not so impressive. He still doesn't make his bed any better than our five year old. He can't quite get his socks in the dirty clothes. So I tell women he's a wonderful man. He's a phenomenal man. But in the end, he's still a man.

But in all seriousness, I am so proud of my husband and I'm excited that he's made the decision to run for president of the United States. That still amazes me.

And although this is my first trip here to New Hampshire, it won't be the last. One of the roles I think that I can play is not just a surrogate campaigner or messenger, but really as a surrogate ear.

Since this is the first time you all have had the opportunity to meet me, I'm going to spend just a little bit of time telling you about me.

I want to share with you how I was brought up—my upbringing, my values, the sort of the things that keep Barack and I grounded—as a way of giving you a sense of how we're going to approach this campaign and how we're going to keep ourselves centered, and how we operate in our lives.

My background is pretty humble. I grew up on the South Side of Chicago in a working class community. A predominantly African American community. My father was a city worker, a blue-collar worker, all of his life. He died a year before I got married.

My mother was a stay at home mom until I went to high school, and I'm the youngest of two. I've got an older brother. My big brother, who I love dearly, Craig, who is now a basketball coach at Brown University and just moved to the east coast, had a great season this year. Yay! Go Bears!

We are both products of the Chicago Public School system. I went to the public schools my entire career. My brother left when he went to high school because he was a scholar athlete, and my parents wanted to make sure he was going to get a good education.

That strategy paid off because he got good grades, and played ball, and earned admission to Princeton University. That was really the first time in my life that I had known somebody who actually got into an Ivy League school. My parents didn't go to college. We had some relatives who had gone to good schools, but that was the first time in my life that I had been exposed to the notion that we could possibly compete and get into a selective Ivy League school.

So when he got in, I thought, well I'm smarter than that guy. So, I applied and I got in as well.

You know, a lot of people ask my brother and I, 'Wow, how did two working class kids wind up at Princeton University?' And for me, what's *not* so remarkable is the fact that we actually got in and thrived, but what I really think about is how my parents managed it all.

How did they afford to send two kids to Princeton? We were there for two years at the same time. I know that they made a great deal of sacrifice, and now looking back, I know just how much they must have sacrificed to make sure that we could achieve our dreams.

When I think about what has shaped me most, it's really my parents. And they're not extraordinary people. They are very ordinary hard working people. But my father, in particular, touches me and my brother the most.

He had multiple sclerosis. He died the year before I got married. For those of you who know anything about MS, it's a degenerative disease and it strikes unexpectedly. My father went from a vibrant athlete in his twenties, served in the military, to not being able to walk or ever run again. He needed the assistance of a cane, and eventually he had to get around on a motorized car.

When I think about my dad, I think about the fact that he never complained once. He never talked about his struggle or his pain. He was never late. He went to work every day. He worked hard. He put every ounce of his energy into taking care of our family.

And what my brother learned from our parents, from my father in particular, was perseverance. We learned consistency. We learned the value of hard work. We learned the value of money. We learned that there's nothing more important than family and community.

And when I think about what really guides me in my life, it's that voice in my head that is my father. And I'm always thinking throughout my life, would this make my father proud? Would he think that I'm living my life to the fullest? Am I making the most of the blessings I've received?"

Chicago, Illinois

Women for Obama Luncheon

April 16, 2007

In her hometown, Michelle addresses a group of women to discuss life as a wife and a mother on the campaign trail.

"This is just a wonderful event. The more I go out, the more I realize that there is something going on. This is a movement! This is something bigger than Barack Obama or Michelle Obama or anyone else in this room. Don't you just feel it? It is amazing. I am honored to be here.

Over the last few months, I've had an opportunity to take a few trips around the country. Some of them, I've gone on with Barack. Most recently, I've been doing trips on my own. We try to take the girls when we can.

The one thing people are most curious about of me— they really want to know, particularly the women, they want to know, 'How are you doing? I mean, *how* are you *doing?*' They really want to know how I'm balancing this stuff. Balancing being a mother, a professional, a campaigner, a wife, a woman... right? And they want to know how things have changed for us over the course of this journey.

What I tell them is that essentially, like many women, I'm doing a whole lot of juggling. Juggling! We all do it. I've found that this period has been both challenging and thrilling at the same time. I've had to cut back on my hours at work... It's okay, I love my job but I have to pick one. That has given me some more time.

With Barack away even more, my focus has been trying to keep my kids sane through all this. That is, first and foremost, for us—making sure Malia and Sasha stay in their routine as much as possible, for as long as possible.

Barack and I measure how well we are doing by asking, 'How are the girls?' And they are just fine. They are going to ballet and gymnastics. They care about the next play date, the next pizza party, and then there is their school. I have to worry about making sure we are on point academically, that we go to all the parent teacher conferences. And Barack still goes to those. It is quite a scheduling feat, but we make it happen. Presentations. School plays. You all know the drill.

I would not be able to do it without this particular table, right here. These are the women in my life: my mother, momma Kay, the girl's godmothers, girlfriends of mine who help me shuttle and keep me held up.

And, at the same time, I'm still trying to find time for myself. Getting the hair done. Yeah, come on. Let's not pretend we don't know that getting the hair and nails done is important—and getting a workout... ladies. That's one of the things I always talk about, gotta exercise. So I am still trying to do that. And to top it all off, I have the pleasure of doing it all in front of the watchful eyes of our friends in the back. Other than that, things haven't changed much.

But seriously, with the exception of the campaign trail and life in the public eye, I have to say that my life now is not really that much different from many of yours. I wake up every morning wondering how on earth I am going to pull off that next minor miracle to get through the day. I know that everybody in this room is going through this. That is the dilemma women face today.

'We've spent the last decade talking a good game about family values, but I haven't seen much in my life that

really shows that we're a society that actually values families.'

Every woman that I know—regardless of race, education, income, background, political affiliation—is struggling to keep her head above water. We try to convince ourselves that somehow doing it all is a badge of honor, but for many of us it is a necessity and we have to be very careful not to lose ourselves in the process.

More often than not, we as women are the primary caretakers in our households—scheduling babysitters, planning play dates, keeping up with regular doctor's appointments. This was my week last week—supervising homework, handing out discipline. Usually, we are the ones in charge of keeping the household together.

I know you men. I know that you guys try to do your part, but the reality is that we're doing it, right? Laundry, cleaning, cooking, shopping, home repairs. You know Barack has my back. He's right there with me, feels my pain, and all that.

And for those of us who work outside of the home as well, we have the additional challenge of coordinating these things with our job responsibilities. How many of us have had to be the ones, when a child gets sick, who is the one to stay home? Or, when a toilet overflows? This was a couple of months ago. I was scrambling around to reschedule being at a 9 o'clock meeting, and Barack, love him to death, put on his clothes and he left!

To top it off, we have the added social pressure of looking good, staying slim. Don't add pounds. Got to look good with wardrobe pulled together. And we have to be in good spirits, right? Ready to be there for our significant others. I'm tired just thinking about it.

These are not challenges that are unique to me. I say this all the time and people think I'm being modest. But the truth is that my experiences tell me that we as women are facing what I call, the next level of challenges. Balancing work, family, and ourselves differently than ever before. My mother says this all the time. She's like, 'I don't know how you do it,' and she means it.

We have made great strides with regards to equality at all levels of society. And because of the struggles so many have fought, many of you right in this room, I know that my daughters can dream big. They really can. There is no ceiling. They can envision themselves anyway that they want: surgeons, Supreme Court justices, basketball stars. They have images that I never had growing up.

I wonder what the unspoken cost that having it all takes on us. If we're scurrying to and from appointments and errands, we don't have a lot of time to take care of our own mental and physical health. For many women, juggling this adds another layer of stress. We see it in our health: women with increased heart attacks, diabetes, asthma. We're up in the numbers and this is no coincidence.

We have to really think through what the next level of challenges are for us. There just aren't enough hours in the day, so we do what we can. What is happening is that we do what we can in spite of the fact that we're not getting the needed support from the government and society as a whole.

The reality is that women and families are not getting the support that they need to thrive. We've spent the last decade talking a good game about family values, but I haven't seen much in my life that really shows that we're a society that actually values families.

We have essentially ignored the plight of women and families. We've told them, 'You go figure it out.' Figure out how you're going to support a family on minimum wage and no benefits. You go figure out who is going to watch your children while you are at work without access to adequate, affordable childcare. You figure out how to keep your family healthy without access to quality health care. Figure out how you're going to ensure that your children get the best education possible. You figure out how you're going to live without access to affordable housing.

Essentially, we've told women, 'Dream big, but after that, you are on your own.'

I'm fortunate because in addition to living in this community, one of the reasons we've stayed based in Chicago is not that we don't like Washington but that my support base is here. And I can't get through my day without it. So, I am blessed. I also know that I have a husband that actually loves me and supports me. Barack and I know that we have been very blessed in our lives, and we don't take anything for granted.

I tease him all the time. You've all heard it. Today, he still didn't put the butter up after he made his breakfast. I said, 'You're just asking for it. You know that I am giving a speech. Why don't you just put the butter up?'

He said he was just giving me material. I said, 'Yeah, right.' He still doesn't make the bed better than Sasha, so I tease him.

But the reality is that my husband is a man who understands my unique struggle and the challenges facing women and families. It is not just because he lives with me—someone who is very opinionated and makes my point.

I am not a martyr, so he hears it.

It is because he actually listens to me and has the utmost respect for my perspective and my life experience.

It is also because he was raised in a household of strong women who he saw struggle and sacrifice for him so he could achieve his dreams.

He saw his grandmother, the primary breadwinner in their household, work her entire life to support their whole family. He saw his mother, a very young, very single parent, trying to finish her education and raise two children across two continents. He sees his sister, a single parent, trying to eke out a life for herself and her daughter on a salary that is much too small.

He sees it in the eyes of women he meets throughout the country. Women who have lost children and husbands in the war.

Women who don't have access to adequate healthcare, to affordable daycare, or to jobs that pay a living wage. Their stories keep him up at night. Their stories, our stories, are the foundation of what guides Barack throughout his life.

And so we are here today, asking you to support us, to join us, to turn those worries into action, to give women hope that there is someone like Barack who is not only decent, trustworthy, compassionate, smart, and hard working, but he is also someone who recognizes that society, our community, is only as strong as our women and our families.

The trick is we can't do this without you. The difference now is that we have this window. That is the beauty of what is going on now. We aren't going to be in this place in four years or eight years. We have the opportunity now. We can be a part of changing the way women are viewed in this country. We can build a government that doesn't just encourage women to dream big but one that provides women and young girls with the support and resources to pursue those dreams.

I want that for my daughters; I want that for your daughters; I want that for this country. I know that we can do it because I believe in Barack. I would not be here otherwise. Too many people know that I wouldn't be here. I believe in his unique ability to bring people together. I see it everywhere I go. This is not an accident, ladies. It is not an accident.

We need you to join us because you know what, Barack, as I tease... he's a wonderful man, he's a gifted man, but in the end, he is just a man. He is an imperfect vessel and I love him dearly.

In all seriousness, he is going to get tired. He is tired now. He is going to make mistakes. He will stumble. Trust me—he will say things that you will not agree with all the time. He will not be able to move you to tears with every word that he says...

That is why this campaign is so important, because it is not *all* about Barack Obama. It is about all of us. It is about us turning these possibilities into action. Women, you know when something is right. You know it. This feels right and it is no accident.

We have the chance today."

Western Iowa

"Be not Afraid"

August 16, 2007

Michelle speaks about their decision to get into the race and the role that fear has played in our country over the past several years.

"Whenever I get in front of an audience, I get pumped up because I'm very passionate about this race. I'm passionate about my husband *in* this race because I know, and I'm trying to convey to you, that there is something very special about this man.

This is why we're doing this—because Barack and I talked long and hard about this decision. You know, this wasn't an easy decision for us because we have two beautiful girls and we have a wonderful life and everything was going fine. There is nothing that would have been more disruptive than a decision to run for president of the United States.

As people talked to us about it, the question that came up again and again, the question that people were most concerned about—they were afraid. It was fear. Fear again raising its ugly head. During one of the most important decisions that we would make—fear. Fear of everything. Fear that we would lose. Fear that we might get hurt. Fear that this would be ugly. Fear that it might hurt our family. Fear.

But you know the reason why I said yes was because I am tired of being afraid. I am tired of living in a country where every decision that we have made over the last ten years wasn't *for* something, but it was because people told us we had to *fear* something.

We had to fear people who looked different from us. Fear people who believed in things that were different from us. Fear of one another right here in our own back yards. I am so tired of fear and I don't want my girls to live in a country, in a world, based on fear.

That's why, and we have to admit, why we are in this war. We are in this [Iraq] war because for eight years, we were told to be afraid.

And everybody followed suit.

Everybody cut and run because it was very unpopular *not* to be afraid—to talk about hope and possibility.

But you know what, there is my husband, who at the time when many people in political life were moving toward fear, he sat on the stage at an anti-war rally, at a time when it wasn't convenient for him to talk in a different unconventional voice. He stood on that stage in the middle of a hotly contested primary in Illinois.

There was a billionaire in the race who was buying up every sign, every politician, and every minister in our state. There was a strong political family in the race. They had been there for years and said there was no way that Barack could build a political machine. There was another black candidate that had been thrown in the race; there was a woman. *Everybody* was in this primary.

Barack Obama was not supposed to win. He couldn't raise the money. He had a strange name. People said, 'Fear him because he's different.'

But even in the midst of all of that, at the core of this race that he could have lost taking a stand, he stood on that stage and he called this war to a tee.

He said, 'This war is wrong. This will cost us billions. We are going after the wrong enemy.'

And it was unpopular, but he was *right*. Because he's special. He's lived a broad life. And the thing I want you all to remember is: please, please, please, don't base your vote this time on fear. Base it on possibility.

Think. Listen.

The game of politics is to make you afraid so that you don't think. And what we need right now isn't political rhetoric. It isn't game playing. We need leadership. We need people with judgment. We need decent people— people with common sense, people with strong family values, people who understand the world.

We need people like Barack Obama who, on the day he is elected to office, will change the way the world sees us. You know that. That is the possibility of Barack Obama.

So, as I introduce to you today my husband, the man who I love, who I'd rather have at home with me, but who I am willing to sacrifice because we have this window of opportunity.

We have a chance to make something real happen— something possible happen—to live beyond our fears.

Think about that and help us.

Help lift us up. Help us fight to change, to transform this country in a fundamental way. This chance won't come around again."

Fairfield, Iowa

Fairfield Convention Center

December 20, 2007

Michelle speaks about her daughters and the future of the children of America.

"I am clear, more now than ever, that we need a Barack Obama presidency right now. Not in four years or in eight years. Right now. We need this to happen right now and I say that because I'm a mother.

I say that because of my girls. Because I love my children deeply. They break my heart. They are my heart and soul. They are the reason I breathe right now and probably will always be.

I think about the kind of country that I want to hand over to them, because that's what we're doing. What we're doing now is preparing the plate that we're going to feed our children from. That's what we're doing.

We're putting the vegetables on. We're making it whole.

So I'm thinking hard about where we are and, quite frankly, I don't think we're anywhere close to where we should be. Not good enough for my girls or for any of our children.

When I think about children, I think about the possibilities. All the things that they can be. We all know that children come to this planet free of bias and bigotry and hate. They are open to anything. Anything is possible. Regardless of race or political affiliation or class. Anything is possible. I want them to live in a nation where they can truly dream of being anything that they want.

Finally, now in 2007, I want my girls to be free. Freedom has nothing to do with race. We are not free if our children are not free to dream. We have to create an environment in this country where every child truly has the potential to be whatever they want to be. And that they will know they have the love, support, and guidance of us all to get there.

I want that for my girls. I want that for all of our children, and we're not there yet. We're nowhere close."

New Hampshire

"To Whom Much is Given, Much is Expected"

January 06, 2008

Michelle delivers a speech in New Hampshire, two days before the New Hampshire primary.

"We're at a point in time in society where life has gotten increasingly harder for folks. I think because of that, it is difficult to reflect on life and to think through these issues because we're all struggling so very, very much just keeping our heads above water. At least regular people are.

And I do consider myself regular people even though I've gone to Princeton and Harvard, and I'm married to a guy who might be the next president of the United States. In my heart of hearts, deep down inside, I'm

27

still that little girl who grew up on the South Side of Chicago.

I'm a product of that experience, through and through. Everything that I think about and do is shaped by the life that I lived in that little apartment above that bungalow, that my father worked so hard to provide for us.

And I remember everyday seeing my father get up and put on that blue uniform and go to that job that I'm sure he didn't love. It was just a blue-collar shift job. No reward. No passion in it.

But the beauty of it was on that little salary, and it must have been small, he was able to care for a family of four: me, my mom, my brother. We lived in this small apartment, and my father could pay his bills and pay them on time. Because he certainly did tell us about that, 'Pay your bills on time.'

That was possible back then, just 43 years ago.

But it wasn't that long ago, that childhood I had, that was very unremarkable in so many ways. People often ask my mother, 'What did you do? What did you feed them? There must have been magic going on in the house.' No. It was a very ordinary life. Very simple, back then. *Way* back then.

But the fact that you could raise a family of four on a single salary today seems remarkable. Maybe the most remarkable thing that I saw growing up was my father's sacrifice and dedication—that hard work. That work ethic.

And as I've told many people, my father was a man with a disability. And I took that for granted because he never complained. Never. Not once.

And I know that he struggled to get up every day and probably lived in fear that one day he wouldn't be able to get up and care for the family that depended on him.

It was a simple kind of life. Father didn't make excuses but he did what he had to do. We could go to the neighborhood school around the corner. We didn't have magnets, charters, all that stuff. You didn't have to sign up for school when you were two in order to get into the one or two decent schools.

We went to the school around the corner. No questions asked. You get up. You go.

And they were decent schools and I talk about that a lot. Because when people look at me, I want them to see the product of public education. I would not be standing here if it weren't for those simple neighborhood schools. Those solid schools with decent teachers. [I am] what an investment in public education can look like. This is what can happen if we do the right thing. Simple.

What I know now, looking back on my life, that *was* remarkable was that a man like my father, on limited means, could send two kids to Princeton. And the pride he must have felt, being able to accomplish all of that. When all of his dreams must have been shattered, put aside, he still had *that*.

That's where he got his pride. That's what gave him his sense of being. And that's true for all Americans all across this country. The story of my father is the story of America.

'We're a nation at war right now, and the only people who are sacrificing are the soldiers—the men and women and their families who are over there.'

Folks don't want much. They just don't want that much. They're not asking for much. People aren't selfish. They aren't naturally greedy. Most folks don't want much. They want to know that if they get up every day and go to work, they'll earn enough to care for their families.

They want to know that their kids can get a decent education at the neighborhood school around the corner. You don't have to drive twelve miles for your kids to get a decent education. And maybe they'll be prepared to go to college if they choose, but if not, they'll be able to get a job and support themselves.

Folks want to know if they get sick, they won't go bankrupt. And that when they're ready to retire after a lifetime of hard work and sacrifice that they'll have a little money in the bank – to be able to live in a little decency. That's all folks want.

But the truth is, that unremarkable life I had all those years ago has become a virtual impossibility today, in 2008. That life is out of reach for so many people. Everyone is struggling. *Everyone* is struggling.

The jobs that my father had don't exist, or they're dwindling all over the country. If you're lucky enough to have that job, your salaries aren't keeping up with the cost of living, so everybody's got to work.

My mom stayed at home until I went to high school because you could do that. Now, if you make that choice, you do it at your family's financial peril. You do. You make huge sacrifices in order to stay home with your kids.

And the public schools around the corner are all so uneven. You go from block to block, neighborhood to neighborhood, and the quality of the school will change dramatically.

No Child Left Behind is sucking the life out of teaching and education in ways that people are echoing all over the country. It's not working.

I know that kids are being tested to death. I have met so many kids who started out loving learning and by the time they're done, they're so sick of tests, that school no longer speaks to their needs.

They're tired. They're deflated.

So now, parents have to worry if the schools they're sending their kids to are preparing them. Then you've got single moms all over the place. Millions of them. Struggling every single day, and every day feeling like they're failing because when you can't get ahead, all you can do is feel like you're failing. All the while being told, 'Your kids aren't where they need to be. You need to be at the parent teacher conference. Why is your kid overweight? You should be chopping up vegetables and making good meals that you can't afford.'

We have made many young mothers feel like they can never get ahead. And college has become out of reach for most families. Kids like me, who've done everything that has been asked of them—studied and prepared, with the hope of going to college—only to get there, look at the cost, and think, 'There's no way I'm going to put my family in this kind of jeopardy for a college education.'

For those who take the risk and make the investment like I did, like my brother did, like Barack did—we come out in four years with so much debt that many of us forgo the careers of our dreams.

We've become a society where we're pricing our young people out of teaching, and social work, and government, and journalism. Anything that is the backbone of this society, the salary won't cover the cost of the education.

Unless you're a hedge fund manager or a corporate lawyer, it's hard to pay your debt off. Barack and I know this. We talk about it all the time. We're just a few years off of paying down our educational debt because we did what we thought we were supposed to do. We didn't stay in corporate America. We went out and worked in the community.

Every job we took, we made less money. My mother was like, 'What is going on with you two?'

We said, 'Mom, we're working for the people.'

She said, 'Yes, but you're broke.' And we were.

The only reason we're out of debt now is because Barack wrote these two bestselling books—which I thank you all for. Thank you for buying the books, because I was sitting around waiting for Barack's trust fund to pop up. I kept looking at him: 'You sure you don't have a trust fund?'

But, we were lucky. We were lucky. There are millions of young couples like us with masters degrees, PhD's, working hard. Barack's other sister is a teacher. She can barely pay off her student loans, and pay for gas, and take care of childcare on her teaching salary.

She is wondering, 'How do I create a future for myself? How do I save for my child's college education when I haven't even paid off my own?'

That's the position many young couples are in. Plus, they are struggling to figure out how to care for their kids. These couples, who have two people working, don't have access to affordable and quality childcare. And if you do, you are not *really* secure about it. There are so many of us mothers who are just agonizing over childcare.

I breathe in and out deeply because of my mother who is 70 years old and retired. She is at home with the girls right now—getting them ready to go to school in the morning.

Good luck, Mom—they've been on vacation for a little while.

There's nothing like Grandma. We have a societal interest in taking care of our seniors. We need them. We need those grandparents around—healthy and secure—to help us. You know. My mom lost her mind. Rules are gone in our house.

She says, 'Why do they have to have vegetables? They don't like vegetables.' What happened to my mother? There is nothing like that kind of love. Having someone there helping you, as a young parent, raise those kids—sharing the values that *you* learned. We need our seniors to be whole, healthy, and in a position financially to contribute.

We're not there. My mom has the pension from my father's job that no longer exists. She is in a financial position to help us, but a lot of our seniors aren't there. This is how we're living in 2008. The beginning of the new year. This is it. I'm not exaggerating. I'm not stretching the truth. I know everybody in this room is dealing with some of what I just said. And it's gotten harder and harder over my lifetime.

Through democratic and republican administrations, it's gotten harder for regular people. There are people who have seen some booms and they've profited. But most regular folks are struggling.

Barack says our greatest challenge as a nation, is not that we're suffering from a deficit of resources, because we're a *wealthy* nation. There is money here. And it's not that we're suffering from a deficit of policies and plans.

The truth is this stuff isn't that complicated on a lot of issues. Take public education. We know what we need to do: it costs money; it requires good teaching; it requires resources and investment. You know how we know? Because there are thousands of excellent public schools all over this country. They exist.

The problem is they don't exist for all children. You have to be one of the lucky ones, living in the right neighborhood with the right parent to get you into the one or two good schools in your community. Everybody else is out of luck.

What Barack says we're suffering from right now is a deficit of empathy. We live in a nation where we have a mutual obligation to one another. Those aren't just words. It's true.

I know in my lifetime, as an adult focusing on this stuff, I don't remember us being asked by our leadership to sacrifice or compromise for one another. I don't remember every being asked.

We're a nation at war right now, and the only people who are sacrificing are the soldiers—the men and women and their families who are over there.

We haven't been asked to pay a tax, to collect a can, to darn a sock. Nothing. In fact, we were told, 'just keep shopping.' It's true.

If we're not directly affected by the war, we're not even *thinking* about it on a daily basis.

That's where we are. What we need is a reminder that we are one another's brothers' and sisters' keepers. That's where we start. We have to sacrifice and compromise for one another. If we live in isolation and we don't know one another, it becomes very difficult to want to compromise for people that you don't think share your values.

We need a different leadership because our souls are broken. We have holes in our souls in ways that I don't think we recognize. We need to be inspired first, to want to be a better nation, to want to treat one another better, to make the sacrifices that are necessary to push us to a different place. I know that so fundamentally.

It's so much more clear to me today than it was even before we got into this race. It's leadership that we need first and foremost.

Folks want to know if they get sick, they won't go bankrupt.

[Barack] learned the values that we're trying to pass on to our daughters. Things like truth and honesty matter in life, all the time. Your word is your bond. When you say you're going to do something, you do it to the best of your ability. And that when you're a working class kid in this society, you don't feel entitled to anything.

You know that you're going to have to work for every single thing. You're going to have to be smarter, faster, better, work harder. You know that. You learn that you treat people with respect and decency, even if you don't know them and even if you don't agree with them. Because that's the right way to treat your neighbor.

We learn that there is nothing more important in this life than commitment to your family and your community. That's why I married Barack Obama. Those values. That is it. He was cute too, that helped.

I knew, with a man like that, I could raise a family with him. I could build a life that would be whole and solid and stable. As I got to know him more, I saw how he struggled to live his values. Not just understand them, but how to make choices with the notion that, 'To whom much is given, much is expected.'

Barack and I, regardless of not having a lot of stuff when we were growing up, we know we were blessed. When you have love and stability and people sacrificing for you, you know you're blessed. You know not every kid gets that.

To whom much is given, much is expected.

When [Barack] graduated from college, he didn't go to work on Wall Street and make a lot of money—which would have helped him pay down his debt. He became a community organizer, working in some of the toughest neighborhoods on the South Side of Chicago, with folks who had reason to be cynical because the government had forgotten a lot of these folks who lived in these neighborhoods.

They had lost their voice and were living in unsafe streets—still are. Barack drove mothers down to City Hall to fight for better schools and safer streets. He worked in those communities for years. Imagine a president of the United States who brings that kind of experience to the Oval Office.

Instead, we give more credit to those who've run corporations or spent years in Washington. I don't know what's wrong with us sometimes. I don't understand it.

To whom much is given, much is expected.

When you have the gift of advocacy, when you are the first African American president of the Harvard Law Review, which Barack was, and you can do anything in the world, you don't give your resources to the most powerful. You don't make money for yourself. You work on issues of justice and fairness."

Los Angeles, California

University of California, Los Angeles

February 2, 2008

Michelle addresses a crowd at UCLA three days before Super Tuesday, when over twenty primary elections will take place.

"This has been an amazing journey. Truly amazing. It has required faith, patience, and sacrifice. It has been one of the most rewarding things I have ever done in my life. It has given me the opportunity to walk into the homes of thousands of Americans across the country to talk, to listen, and to be reminded that there is truly more that unites us than divides us.

We are so close in this country to being a *United* States. People ask me how I feel throughout this journey and I tell them, every single day I am thinking about my girls, Malia and Sasha.

I do this because of them. In America we all love our children. We love our children. They break our hearts. We want them to be able to dream of anything for themselves. I want my girls to travel this world with pride.

I believe that in 2008, we should be in a place where children can believe in any kind of life for themselves, regardless of their race, their gender, their socio-economic status. They should be able to dream their dreams and know they have the love and resources of this entire nation behind them. That is the least that we can do for our children. But in 2008, we are not there yet.

We live in isolation and because of that isolation we fear one another. We don't know our neighbors. We don't talk. We believe that our pain is our own. We don't realize that the struggles and challenges of all of us are the same.

We are too isolated and we are a nation that is still too cynical. Particularly young people. They say you won't vote. They say you won't vote.

They say it because they believe that, like many Americans, you will fold your arms in disgust and look at this process as if it's someone else's problem. We look at it as 'them and they' as opposed to 'us'. We don't engage because we are still too cynical.

'You are better than anybody's limited expectations of you.'

There is still a level of meanness in this culture. And as a mother raising two girls, trust me, I don't want them to be mean girls. I want them to understand that we can talk to one another civilly.

In this society, we sometimes mistake toughness for meanness. We like tough talk. We pass that on to our children, and I don't want that for my girls.

We are still a nation that is too guided by fear. We have become afraid of everyone and everything. The problem with fear is that it clouds our judgment. It cuts us off. It cuts us off from one another in our own homes, in our own communities. It has certainly cut us off from the rest of the world.

The problem with fear is that it creates a veil of impossibility, and we spend more time in this society talking about what won't work, what we can't do, what won't happen. The problem is we pass that on to our children.

We are creating a generation of young people who are doubtful. They are hesitant. They are insular. They don't try because someone already told them why they can't do it.

I don't want that for my girls. I don't want that for any of our children.

Part of the problem and the challenge is that when you are a nation that is struggling everyday, which most regular folks are, it is hard to move out of the isolation, to move away from the fear.

I know that we are a nation that is struggling. I look at how America has become increasingly difficult for everyday American folks.

You can't stay home with your kids because you need one, two, and three salaries. And don't be a single parent in this county. There are millions of them, feeling like failures because they can't keep up on a single parent salary. You can't go to parent teacher conferences, you can't do homework with your kids, make sure they stay out of trouble. Not in America if you're a single parent.

And college has become a dream. Many of you here at UCLA are here because you did everything that you were asked to do. You were like millions of kids who did their homework, studied, and prepared, and got admitted, looked at the cost of college and said, I can't do this. For those of us who took the chance and took the loans, we will find ourselves, in five or six years, so mired in debt that we have to give up the career of our dreams.

In America, you can't become a teacher or a nurse. The cost of the degree is more than the salary that you'll earn.

And don't get sick in this country. Not here. Americans are in debt, not because they live frivolously, but because someone got sick.

Even with insurance, the deductibles and treatments are so high that people are still putting services and medications on credit cards. They can't get out from under it. I can go on and on and on, but this is how we're living in 2008.

The question in this campaign is not whether Barack Obama is ready. The question is what are *we* ready for?

Barack Obama will require you to work. He is going to demand that you shed your cynicism, that you put down your division, that you come out of your isolation, that you move out of your comfort zones, that you push yourselves to be better, and that you *engage*.

Barack will not allow you to go back to your lives as usual—uninvolved, uninformed. You will have to stay at the seat of the table of democracy. Not just on Tuesday, but in a year from now, in four years from now, in eight years from now—you will have to be engaged.

You will have to be engaged and we are going to need you. I hold no level of fear in this race because there is no expectation that we are doing this alone.

We will need all of you standing with us, praying us, working with us every step of the way, because that's how change happens in this country.

Dreams and inspiration are everything.

If it weren't for a little dreaming, I wouldn't be here. I was that ten year old little girl. I am not supposed to be here. I wasn't supposed to go to Princeton because someone told me my test scores weren't high enough. I wasn't supposed to go to Harvard Law School because they said it would be too much for me.

Every step of the way in my life, and so many of you out there have been told, 'No. Don't. We're not ready. Wait your turn.' All the while, knowing in your heart, that you are better than anybody's limited expectations of you.

If we don't learn anything else through this race, I want young people out there to understand if they push past other people's limited expectations of them and reach for their seats at the table, that others feel so entitled to, when they get to that table, they are going to find that they are just as ready, just as qualified, just as capable as anyone sitting around that table.

Those doubts and fears that we fester in this society, those are a lie.

We need to do a little dreaming. Dream of a day when a man like Barack Obama is standing in front of the capital, with his hand on the Bible, taking the oath of office to become the next president of the United States. Just imagine what message that image will send to all of the kids in this nation.

If we can do that here in this nation, imagine what we can do around the world. We all know the world is watching. We have young kids all over the world who are looking at this nation, trying to figure out who we are and what we want to become.

We have a chance not just to make history, but we can change the world. We can change the world. Yes we can. Yes we can. Yes we can..."

Milwaukee, Wisconsin

"First time Proud"

February 18, 2008

This speech became the subject of much controversy in the press and a target for political opponents.

"What we have learned over this year is that hope is making a comeback. It is making a comeback. And let me tell you something, for the first time in my adult lifetime, I am really proud of my country. And not just because Barack has done well, but because I think people are hungry for change.

And I have been desperate to see our country moving in that direction and just not feeling so alone in my frustration and disappointment. I've seen people who are hungry to be unified around some basic common issues, and it's made me proud.

I feel privileged to be a part of all of this. Travelling around to states all over this country and being reminded that there is more that unites us than divides us, that the struggles of a farmer in Iowa are no different than what's happening on the South Side of Chicago; that people are feeling the same pain and wanting the same things for their families."

Rhode Island

Campaign event

February 20, 2008

Michelle makes it clear that she is, in fact, proud of her country.

"Let me tell you something, I *am* proud. I'm proud of this country and I'm proud of the fact that people are ready to roll up their sleeves and do something phenomenal. I know I wouldn't be here, standing here, Barack and I's stories wouldn't be possible if it weren't for a fundamental belief and pride in this country and what it stands for.

We are just truly moved by what we've been seeing this year. It is not all about Barack. It is about people's hopes and desires. And that moves me.

I say this time and time again. We aren't doing this for ourselves. This isn't about us. It's about the future. It's about our children.

I think about my girls every single day when I'm out here on the campaign trail. Everywhere I go I am thinking about them. About their day to day concerns, their cares, are they happy, am I a good parent? Am I feeding them right? Teaching them good lessons?

I worry all the time and I know you all are in the same position."

Indianapolis, Indiana

Town Hall Meeting with Barack

April 30, 2008

Barack and Michelle sit with a small group of supporters. Michelle speaks briefly about the struggles American families are facing.

"For most of my lifetime, I've felt disconnected from Washington. When decisions are made and things happen, you're sort of left at your kitchen table scratching your head and wondering, well, who is that supposed to help? Because it doesn't reflect the reality on the ground.

Part of me says that maybe it's because the further up you go [in politics] and longer you're gone, the harder it is to remember the struggles on the ground.

We're just coming out of those struggles. Not just because we're a young couple with small kids, with all of the emotions and challenges and the struggles that come with raising kids, like being a working mom.

Barack and I have had interesting conversations about not just our share in the household, but what burden that has on me, trying to hold down a job. Because you need to do that to pay off your loan debt and keep up on the bills, even when you've got great degrees like we do.

Work isn't a choice. It never felt like a choice to me. But I never felt like I was doing anything 100% right.

You're divided among so many different needs: trying to be a good mother, a good wife, trying to keep your marriage together, trying to make sure you're healthy, trying to make sure your kids are loved and cared for.

Those stresses tend to eat up families in ways I don't think we even acknowledge.

The lack of quality, affordable childcare is critical to the health and wellbeing of our communities. It's not an option. Having decent public education—I am a product of public education. One of the reasons my parents were able to do what they did, is they didn't need to set aside money for private schools because the public schools around the corner were decent.

MICHELLE OBAMA

Now every family is struggling to make sure their kids are in a good school. How do you get in the system? Do you live in the right place? Is No Child Left Behind doing what it needs to do? Will they be able to compete and get into college?

There is a lot of work to do.

I am the cynic in the family. [Barack] is the hope guy. I've seen it. I'm like, 'You really do believe this stuff, don't you?' And it's a good thing because I have spent my life trying to convince him not to be a politician. Teach, write, sing, dance. I don't care what you do; just don't do this. These people are mean.

He has always said, from the time we met, that in his experience most people are decent. Most people want the same things, but we get lost in our division and our isolation.

Barack says if you could find a leader to unite people around values and do a little truth telling, that the American people can handle tough truth. And with a little courage, that they would be ready to sacrifice, if they felt that the sacrifice was to a greater good. And that's what we've been seeing.

New York, New York

Democratic National Committee's Gay and Lesbian Leadership Council

June 27, 2008

Michelle speaks on the Obamas' view of "The world as it should be."

"I am honored to be with you in a week that reminds us just how far we've come as a country. Five years ago today, the Supreme Court delivered justice with the decision of Lawrence versus Texas.

That case stated that same sex couples would never again be persecuted through the use of criminal law. And on Saturday, we recognized the anniversary of the day people stood up at Stonewall and said, enough.

These anniversaries remind us that no matter who we are, or where we come from, or what we look like, we are only here because of the brave efforts of those who came before us—that we are all only here because of those who marched and bled and died.

From Selma to Stonewall, in a pursuit of that more perfect Union, that is the Promise of this country.

Over the course of this campaign, we've seen a fundamental change in the level of political engagement in this country. We've seen this renewed sense of possibility and a hunger for change like I've never seen before. We've seen people of all ages and backgrounds investing time and energy like never before.

We've seen people talking with their neighbors about candidates, and issues, and super delegates—working hard to clarify misperceptions—challenging one another, not just to think differently about this country, but about the world and our place in that world.

It's precisely this type of individual engagement and investment that has been the mission of Barack's life. Barack has always believed that there is more that unites us than divides us, that our common stories and struggles and values are what make this country great, that meaningful change never happens from the top down but from the bottom up.

I'll never forget the first time that I realized there was something special about Barack. It was in that summer that I was mentoring Barack, about twenty years ago. We were just getting to know one another.

I was his advisor and he wanted to take me out on a date... I wasn't having any of that. He tried and tried and eventually, he wanted me to get to know him better by introducing me to the work that he felt defined who he was—his work as a community organizer.

He took me to a small church basement where people were gathered. He spoke eloquently about what he saw as 'the world as it is' and 'the world as it should be.'

He said the key to change is understanding that our job, as citizens of this nation, is to work hard each and every day to narrow the gap between those two ideas.

He explained that we often settle for the world as it is, even when it doesn't reflect our personal values. He reminded us that it's only through determination and hard work that we slowly make 'the world as it is' and 'the world as it should be,' one in the same.

His words challenged each of us to believe in ourselves.

In his first year in the Illinois State Senate, Barack co-sponsored a bill amending the Illinois human rights act to include protections of LGBT men and women. He worked on that bill for seven years, serving as the chief co-sponsor and lobbying his colleagues to reject the political expedience of homophobia and to make LGBT equality a priority in our state.

In 2004, his efforts paid off when that bill finally became law, prohibiting discrimination on the basis of sexual orientation and gender identity in the workplace, in housing, and in all public places.

He stood up, in 2004, at the Democratic National Convention and told all of America that we refuse to be divided anymore. That's the choice in this election. Between slipping backward and moving forward; those are our choices. Between being timid or being courageous; those are our choices. Between fighting for the world as it should be or settling for the world as it is; those are our choices.

My husband is running for president to build an America that lives up to the ideals written in our constitution.

We've just come through this historic primary election where a *woman* and a *black* man, through this historic primary, could have been president of the United States. That, in and of itself, shows movement in this country.

Believe me this road hasn't been painless. Not at all. But you know change never is painless. Change is not easy.

As I travel across this country, I am certain that we have arrived at a moment in our collective history where we are ready to move forward.

We are ready. We're ready to create that world as it should be.

All across this country, people are hungry for this, but he can't do it alone. [Barack] says change happens when ordinary people are ready to take the reins of their own destiny.

He needs you by his side every step of the way. That kind of change isn't going to be easy. Nothing that we have to do over the next four or eight years is going to be easy. There will be powerful forces who believe that things should stay just as they are, that everything is fine.

That's where you all come in. Your voices of truth and hope and possibility have got to drown out the skeptics and the cynics. If you stand with my husband, if you reach for what is possible, and if you refuse to let this chance get away, we can begin building that better world in November.

Thank you so much."

Chicago, Illinois

Women for Obama Lunch Reception

July 28, 2008

Michelle discusses the stories and struggles she's heard on the campaign and explains how her husband, Barack Obama, plans to address them.

"We all have to be united. In fact, we are all united. This lunch is a representation of that. Because we know the importance of women's voices and votes in this election, we're going to decide the outcome of this race. Whether the bad guys or the good guys win, it's going to be up to us.

And our vote is only growing. In 2000, 50% of voters were women. In 2004, women made up 54% of the vote. And in this election, we'll make up an even greater percentage of the vote. That's why Women for

Obama, and your involvement, is going to be critical for this year.

Women for Obama's core principle is simple: it's all about connecting women. It's about women talking to women all over this country—sharing their stories, telling people about this guy Barack Obama. It's about people educating one another on the issues, talking about our world and our place in this world.

There has been a core group of Women for Obama supporters that are 30,000 strong—30,000 women who make this happen.

Let me just tell you a little bit about what that group has done over the last year and a half. Four thousand women have traveled and actually embedded themselves in states all over this country to help organize and get out the vote. Four thousand women have changed their lives and slept on floors on behalf of this campaign.

We've hosted 3,500 house parties all over this country. Some of those were Girl's Night Out parties that helped to connect younger women to this effort. We've made over 200,000 phone calls and written 250,000 post cards, often to undecided women, particularly to older women who might not connect to the campaign through the online process.

Nearly 300 women related groups have started sites on our web. They've included everything from Pennsylvania Women for Obama to Women Business Owners for Obama, and then... there are Obama's Mamas. That's an older group of women who are supporting my husband.

It's this woman-to-woman connection that has been effective. We haven't just lumped women in with other special interest groups; we've actually connected our women to other supporters who are undecided.

It's real work. We've got business women talking to business women, seniors talking to seniors, moms talking to other moms.

All of this, believe it or not, comes from Barack Obama. He wants every single American to have an ownership stake in this campaign. A bottom up approach. The only way you do that is people buying in and working hard.

Of the thirty-five states that held primaries, Barack won the women's vote in fifteen of those states.

So there's something going on. We're doing something right, but we have more work to do.

We need to educate more women and bring them into this campaign. They need to know about this candidate. Then we have to get them to vote. Because if there's one thing I've seen out there, it's that women need an advocate in the White House now more than ever before.

Like all of you, I wear a whole lot of hats. Lots of hats going on. I'm a working woman. I'm a daughter. I'm a sister. I'm a best friend. But the one role that I cherish the most, that you've come to know, is that role of mom.

My girls are the first thing I think about when I wake up in the morning and the last thing I think about before I go to bed. And I don't care where I am. On the campaign trail, at a fundraiser—I am worried about how my girls are doing, about their wellbeing, about their stability.

So for me, policies that support working women and families—this is *personal*. These are the issues that I carry in my heart every single day.

I'm always amazed at how different things are for working women and families today than when I was growing up. When I was a kid, my father, a blue-collar worker, was able to go to work and earn enough to support a family of four while my mother stayed home with me and my brother.

But today, living with one income like we did, especially a shift worker's income like my dad's, just doesn't cut it anymore. People can't do it. Most families in this country are finding that both parents *have* to work. Have to—it's not a choice.

And it's even harder if you're a single parent. Often times, they work more than one job to make ends meet. And that doesn't include the jobs that happen when you come home from work. Those jobs, quite frankly, that still fall predominantly on the laps of women: getting the laundry done, making dinner, handing out discipline, getting the homework done, paying the bills.

And as you see the bills piling up and the money running short, then you've got another job: late night worrier.

There are just not enough hours in the day.

Like many of you, I have spent my nights wishing for that magic machine that could add more hours to the day so I could sleep a little longer—something that could clone me so that I could be in two, three places at one time, at least.

I don't know about you, but I haven't found that machine. It hasn't shown up. But even with that—I joke about our challenges—Barack and I know that we are lucky.

We've got the resources and support we need to get through. I'm particularly lucky because I have *my* mom, Marian Robison. This is the woman who keeps me grounded, who stays at home with my girls and makes sure that they're okay. Mom, I love you.

All of us in this room are lucky. But as I've traveled this country over the past year and a half, I've met countless working moms and dads who aren't so fortunate.

Over the past year and a half, I have been holding working women's roundtables all across the country in almost every state that I've been in. These sessions have given me an opportunity to hear first-hand about the challenges facing working women and their families.

'I realized that if that's the kind of world I want for my girls, I had to do everything in my power, make every sacrifice to make it possible.'

During a roundtable in Pontiac, Michigan, I heard from a fifty-seven year-old widow who lost her job due to an illness and couldn't pay her own medical bills.

She helps pay for childcare for her grandchildren while her daughter works multiple jobs. During that roundtable, she expressed great shame and embarrassment. This is how people are feeling: shame and embarrassment because, despite a lifetime of hard work and sacrifice, she is still finding herself in a position where she can't make ends meet.

She told me, 'It's degrading.' She feels degraded by her struggle.

In Kansas City, I heard from a forty year-old single mother with two daughters and a seventeen month-old granddaughter. She makes $75,000 a year, but her student loans costs are $100,000. She said that it will take her twenty or thirty years to pay off that loan debt, making payments of $700 or $800 per month.

The crowd gasped when they heard that, but this is the norm when you have educational debt.

On top of that, she faces soaring health care costs for her own mother's illness. Now this woman did everything that society asked of her—everything. Even though she had children at a young age, she worked hard, held down a job, she never gave up. She went back to college and got her MBA, which is the result of her debt. She is working in a wonderful job, but she still can't make ends meet.

She says that she and her girls don't live extravagantly. She said their one pleasure was to go out maybe once a week to Taco Tuesday and have dinner out.

She said they can't do that anymore. Maybe, if they're lucky, they can go out once a month or so. But even with all of that, what does she say? She says, 'I'm blessed,' which is how Americans feel.

She said, 'I'm blessed, and I don't know how people do it who don't have what I have.' In her own struggle, she is worried about others.

And I heard from a nun, Sister Berta. She has a non-profit that cares for 500 children through a day care service. She works a lot with foster kids and mothers struggling to keep their lives together. She said that the mothers try so hard. They're working at fast food joints, making beds at hotels and hospitals, but they just can't save and they can't afford rent.

At that very same discussion, there was another working mom. She had a good job at a medical company but she still couldn't afford childcare for her only son. She was lucky to have a family member her son could stay home with.

She worried because her doctor said her son has some developmental issues and could benefit from being in a more social environment, and that she should put him in daycare. But she can't afford it. So she's worried that because she can't afford daycare, her son is missing out.

The beautiful thing at that roundtable was that afterwards, Sister Berta came up and offered this woman childcare—to take in her son at ten dollars a week.

I hear these stories everywhere I go from women doing everything that's asked of them. And these women aren't asking for much. They're not asking for government to solve all their problems. They're willing to work. They're just hoping that Washington will understand what's happening to our families, particularly mothers and the variety of challenges they face.

And there just aren't enough Sister Bertas out there in the world to catch those who don't make it and fall through the cracks. These struggles, the struggles of working women and families, are just not new to me or to any of us, and they're certainly not new to Barack.

Barack is the product of this kind of strong woman upbringing, struggling to make it together. Barack has been shaped by these stories.

He grew up with a mother who was a young, single woman who struggled to finish her education and take care of him and his sister.

She was one of the kindest people that you'd ever meet. She was a dreamer. The kind of person who would hop on the back of motorcycles to help women in rural credit programs all around the world. She had this eternal optimism and commitment to fairness and justice, an unwavering belief she could help bring about a better life for women all over the world.

A lot of her still lives in Barack. It explains a lot, if you know what I mean.

She was determined to show him and his sister that in America, there are no barriers to success if you're willing to work hard. But he also saw her struggle. Often times, needing to rely on food stamps to pay the bills.

In her final months, stricken with cancer, he saw her worrying more about how she would pay her medical bills than about getting well.

He saw his grandmother, the primary breadwinner for his family, work her way up at a bank. But he also saw her unable to break certain glass ceilings—watching men who were less qualified and less prepared than her, soar passed her.

And he sees me, his wife, trying to juggle it all, in the midst of it. Always living with the guilt that if I'm spending too much time at work, then I'm not giving enough time to my girls.

And if I'm with my girls, then I'm shortchanging work. Or...you name it. It's a guilt that we all live with in this room; can I hear an Amen?

I have spent my nights wishing for that magic machine that could add more hours to the day so I

MICHELLE OBAMA

could sleep a little longer—something that could clone me so that I could be in two, three places at one time, at least.

I know you all understand this guilt. Barack understands it too because the women he loves most in the world have gone through this. That's why he carries our stories, and the stories of women who've struggled, with him every day.

And that's why as president, Barack will change Washington so that we're not just talking about family values; we actually are creating policies that show that we value families in this country.

That's why today, we're unveiling what I'm calling the Blueprint; our plan to support working women and families. There's not enough time today to go through it all, but I encourage you all to read through it and share it with others.

It lays out my husband's policies that make it easier for working parents to support, care for, and raise their families; policies that encourage healthy families; policies that no longer force working women to choose between their kids and their careers.

He'll expand the Family and Medical Leave Act, so that millions of women will be able to take time off to care for a baby or an elderly parent—or just have a few hours to attend a parent teacher conference, or take a child to the doctor. He'll require employers to provide all their workers with at least seven paid sick days a year so women don't get punished just because someone gets sick or has a family emergency.

He'll keep fighting to ensure that women are paid fairly for their hard work by closing the gap that exists when tens of millions of working women who are the primary breadwinners for their families, but still earn just 77 cents for every dollar men earn.

And because one in four women will still experience domestic violence in her lifetime, Barack is committed to continuing to focus resources for prevention and support to affected families. That's why he helped reauthorize the Violence Against Women Act in the U.S. Senate, and that's why as president, he will continue those efforts.

And he'll restore fairness to our economy, ensure a world class education for our kids, and create quality, affordable health care for everyone who wants it. Because until we do all that, the choices women are forced to make won't get any easier.

As many of you in this room know, when Barack first talked about running for president, my initial reaction was something like, 'No, please don't do this!' You see, I thought politics was a mean, rough business. Eh.

And honestly, the last thing in the world I wanted was to turn my girls' lives upside down in the midst of all of this. To have them hear their parents being criticized on TV, to have their dad be away from them for weeks on end. I didn't want that for my girls. I don't think anyone would really want that for their kids.

But then I took a step back and started thinking about the world I want to hand over to my daughters. I had to think long and hard about wanting them to be able to dream of anything for themselves. You know, wanting them to be able to imagine any kind of future for themselves, and know that they would have the kind of support from this country that would allow them and all of our children to achieve those dreams.

And then I realized that if that's the kind of world I want for my girls, I had to do everything in my power, make every sacrifice to make it possible.

So that's why I'm a Woman for Obama. That is why. Because I believe that helping Barack become president is the best investment I could ever make in my daughters' futures—and in all our children's futures.

Because I want my daughters, and all our sons and daughters, to have opportunities that we and our mothers and grandmothers could only dream of.

So, we're just about three months away from making those dreams a reality. Can you believe it? We wouldn't be at this point without you. But we have a lot of work to do, and we need your help.

With courage and passion, faith and hope, and possibility, we can change not just this country, but maybe even the world.

Thank you, so much.

Section 2

This section includes speeches given by Michelle Obama during the general presidential election: August of 2008 through October of 2008. Speeches are in sequential order.

Denver, Colorado

"One Nation"

August 25, 2008

Michelle Obama's speech from the Democratic National Convention

"As you might imagine, for Barack, running for president is nothing compared to that first game of basketball with my brother Craig.

I can't tell you how much it means to have Craig and my mom here tonight. Like Craig, I can feel my dad looking down on us, just as I've felt his presence in every grace filled moment of my life.

At 6-foot-6, I've often felt like Craig was looking down on me too... literally. But the truth is, both when we were kids and today, he wasn't looking down on me; he was watching over me.

And he's been there for me every step of the way since that clear February day nineteen months ago, when—with little more than our faith in each other and a hunger for change—we joined my husband, Barack Obama, on the improbable journey that has led us to this moment.

But each of us also comes here tonight by way of our own improbable journey. I come here tonight as a sister, blessed with a brother who is my mentor, my protector, and my lifelong friend.

And I come here as a wife who loves my husband and believes he will be an extraordinary president.

And I come here as a mom whose girls are the heart of my heart and the center of my world. They're the first thing I think about when I wake up in the morning and the last thing I think about when I go to bed at night. Their future, and all our children's future, is my stake in this election.

And I come here as a daughter—raised on the South Side of Chicago by a father who was a blue-collar city worker and a mother who stayed at home with my brother and me. My mother's love has always been a sustaining force for our family. And one of my greatest joys is seeing her integrity, her compassion, and her intelligence reflected in my own daughters.

My Dad was our rock. Although he was diagnosed with multiple sclerosis in his early thirties, he was our provider, our champion, our hero. But as he got sicker, it got harder for him to walk; it took him longer to get dressed in the morning. But if he was in pain, he never let on. He never stopped smiling and laughing, even while struggling to button his shirt, even while using two canes to get himself across the room to give my mom a kiss. He just woke up a little earlier, and worked a little harder.

He and my mom poured everything they had into me and Craig. It was the greatest gift a child could receive: never doubting for a single minute that you're loved and cherished and have a place in this world.

And thanks to their faith and their hard work, we both were able to go on to college. So I know firsthand from their lives and mine that the American Dream endures.

And you know, what struck me when I first met Barack was that even though he had this funny name, even though he'd grown up all the way across the continent in Hawaii, his family was so much like mine. He was raised by grandparents who were working class folks just like my parents, and by a single mother who struggled to pay the bills just like we did.

Like my family, they scrimped and saved so that he could have opportunities that they never had for themselves. And Barack and I were raised with so many of the same values: that you work hard for what you want in life, that your word is your bond, and you do what you say you're going to do, that you treat people with dignity and respect, even if you don't know them and even if you don't agree with them.

Barack and I set out to build lives guided by these values and to pass them on to the next generation. Because we want our children, and all children in this nation, to know that the only limit to the height of your achievements is the reach of your dreams and your willingness to work for them.

And as our friendship grew, and I learned more about Barack. He introduced me to the work he'd done when he first moved to Chicago after college. You see, instead of going to Wall Street, Barack had gone to work in neighborhoods devastated when steel plants shut down and jobs dried up. And he'd been invited back to speak to people from those neighborhoods about how to rebuild their community.

The people gathered together that day were ordinary folks doing the best they could to build a good life. See, they were parents trying to get by paycheck to paycheck, grandparents trying to get by on a fixed income, men frustrated that they couldn't support their families after their jobs disappeared. Those folks weren't asking for a handout or a shortcut. They were ready to work. They wanted to contribute. They believed, like you and I believe, that America should be a place where you can make it if you try.

And Barack stood up that day and spoke words that have stayed with me ever since. He talked about 'the world as it is' and 'the world as it should be.' And he said that all too often, we accept the distance between the two, and we settle for the world as it is—even when it doesn't reflect our values and aspirations.

But he reminded us that we also know what our world *should* look like. He said we know what fairness and justice and opportunity look like. And he urged us to believe in ourselves—to find the strength within ourselves to strive for the world as it should be. And isn't that the Great American Story?

It's the story of men and women gathered in churches and union halls and high school gyms; people who stood up and marched and risked everything they had, refusing to settle, determined to mold our future into the shape of our ideals.

It is because of their will and determination that this week, we celebrate two anniversaries: the 88th anniversary of women winning the right to vote and the 45th anniversary of that hot summer day when Dr. King lifted our sights and our hearts with his dream for our nation.

I stand here today at the crosscurrents of that history knowing that my piece of the American Dream is a blessing hard won by those who came before me. All of them driven by the same conviction that drove my dad to get up an hour early each day to painstakingly dress himself for work. The same conviction that drives the men and women I've met all across this country:

People who work the day shift kiss their kids goodnight and head out for the night shift—without disappointment, without regret—see that goodnight kiss as a reminder of everything they're working for.

The military families who say grace each night with an empty seat at the table, the servicemen and women who love this country so much, they leave those they love most to defend it.

The young people across America serving our communities, teaching children, cleaning up neighborhoods, caring for the least among us each and every day.

People like Hillary Clinton, who put those 18 million cracks in the glass ceiling, so that our daughters and our sons can dream a little bigger and aim a little higher.

People like Joe Biden, who's never forgotten where he came from and never stopped fighting for folks who work long hours and face long odds and need someone on their side again.

All of us driven by a simple belief that the world as it is just won't do, that we have an obligation to fight for the world as it should be.

And that is the thread that connects our hearts. That is the thread that runs through my journey and Barack's journey and so many other improbable journeys that have brought us here tonight, where the current of history meets this new tide of hope.

That is why I love this country.

'[My dad] and my mom poured everything they had into me and Craig. It was the greatest gift a child could receive: never doubting for a single minute that you're loved and cherished and have a place in this world.'

And in my own life, in my own small way, I've tried to give back to this country that has given me so much. That's why I left a job at a law firm for a career in public service, working to empower young people to volunteer in their communities. Because I believe that each of us—no matter what our age or background or walk of life—each of us has something to contribute to the life of this nation.

It's a belief Barack shares—a belief at the heart of his life's work.

See, it's what he did all those years ago, on the streets of Chicago: setting up job training to get people back to work and afterschool programs to keep kids safe, working block by block to help people lift up their families.

It's what he did in the Illinois Senate: moving people from welfare to jobs, passing tax cuts for hard working families, and making sure women get equal pay for equal work. It's what he's done in the United States Senate: fighting to ensure that the men and women who serve this country are welcomed home, not just with medals and parades, but with good jobs and benefits and health care—including mental health care.

See, that's why he's running: to end the war in Iraq responsibly, to build an economy that lifts every family, to make sure health care is available for every American, and to make sure every child in this nation has a world class education all the way from preschool to college. That's what Barack Obama will do as president of the United States of America.

He'll achieve these goals the same way he always has—by bringing us together and reminding us how much we share and how alike we really are. You see, Barack doesn't care where you're from, or what your background is, or what party, if any, you belong to. That's not how he sees the world. He knows that thread that connects us: our belief in America's Promise, our commitment to our children's future. He knows that that thread is strong enough to hold us together as one nation even when we disagree.

It was strong enough to bring hope to those neighborhoods in Chicago. It was strong enough to bring hope to the mother he met, worried about her child in Iraq; hope to the man who's unemployed, but can't afford gas to find a job; hope to the student working nights to pay for her sister's health care, sleeping just a few hours a day.

And it was strong enough to bring hope to people who came out on a cold Iowa night and became the first voices in this chorus for change, that has been echoed by millions of Americans from every corner of this nation: millions of Americans who know that Barack understands their dreams; millions of Americans who know that Barack will fight for people like them, and that Barack will finally bring the change we need.

And in the end, and in the end after all that's happened these past nineteen months, the Barack Obama I know today is the same man I fell in love with nineteen years ago.

He's the same man who drove me and our new baby daughter home from the hospital ten years ago this summer, inching along at a snail's pace, peering anxiously at us in the rearview mirror, feeling the whole weight of her future in his hands, determined to give her everything he'd struggled so hard for himself, determined to give her something he never had: the affirming embrace of a father's love.

And as I tuck that little girl and her little sister into bed at night, I think about how one day, they'll have families of their own. And one day, they—and your sons and daughters—will tell their own children about what we did together in this election. They'll tell them how this time, we listened to our hopes instead of our fears. How this time, how this time, we decided to stop doubting and to start dreaming. How this time, in this great country—where a girl from the South Side of Chicago can go to college and law school, and the son of a single mother from Hawaii can go all the way to the White House—that we committed ourselves. We committed ourselves to building the world as it should be.

So tonight, in honor of my father's memory and my daughters' future—out of gratitude for those whose triumphs we mark this week and those whose everyday sacrifices have brought us to this moment— let us devote ourselves to finishing their work. Let us work together to fulfill their hopes, and let us stand together to elect Barack Obama president of the United States of America.

Thank you. God bless you. And God bless America."

Denver, Colorado

Democratic National Convention

August 25, 2008

Michelle gives a surprise speech at the "Chicago Night" event at the Democratic National Convention.

"It was a great night. Not just for the Obama family, but for the nation. And I would not miss being here to say hello to all of you, all of our friends, people who have had our backs for years and years and years— many of you really taking and making some hard decisions to support this campaign.

Just know that Barack and I are going to work very hard to make you proud. Because one thing I know after watching how Barack has handled himself throughout this entire nineteen months, is that he is more than ready to be Commander in Chief. So we just need to do our part now.

We need to register people to vote. We need to go back to our states. And if we've got Illinois all taken care of, then we need to go to Michigan and Iowa and Ohio and Minnesota, and make our voices heard.

When people know who Barack Obama is, and what our vision is, and when they understand what our family stands for, people get it.

And you guys probably know us better than anyone. You have seen us in and out of Chicago and Illinois, and you can vouch for what we believe in. So we're counting on you. Keep us in your prayers. Keep having our backs and we will do our part.

I want to thank you guys for letting me stop by. Take care."

Santa Fe, New Mexico

College of Santa Fe

September 4, 2008

Michelle addresses military spouses during a roundtable discussion.

"It's a pleasure to be here, and it's an honor to visit a state that's given so many of its sons and daughters to protecting our nation in the military. Today more than 1500 troops from New Mexico are serving in Iraq and Afghanistan. Since 911, more than 4000 members of New Mexico's National Guard have been called up for everything from homeland security to overseas combat. One-hundred and eighty-thousand veterans call New Mexico home.

Not far from here, where we meet more than 42,000 men and women who served our country with honor, buried in the Santa Fe National Cemetery.

I know that today we're all thinking about the troops, as we talk about the families, who they are thinking about every single day. They're on our minds and in our hearts every single day.

One of the things that I've enjoyed most during the last nineteen months that I've been out on the campaign trail is holding these kinds of roundtable discussions with military spouses. These conversations have given me the opportunity to hear their stories— your stories about your lives, your families, the unique challenges that you face.

They are not asking government to solve all their problems... They're just asking for a Washington that understands and recognizes the challenges that military families face as part of their extraordinary commitment to our country.

What I say to every spouse I meet is that I don't think the rest of America is aware of the challenges that these families are facing. One thing that's very clear from these conversations, though, is the pride that these families feel in this country. Pride not just in this country but also in their families. The pride in the service the family is giving and to the loved ones who are serving the United States.

Indeed, your pride is well deserved. I'm honored to be here with all of you. Barack and I and all Americans are so grateful for the sacrifices that you are making every single day.

My job here today is relatively easy over the jobs that I've had over the last nineteen months. I'm here to listen. Then, I'm going to take these stories back. I will remember every single one of them and take them back so that they become a part of guiding policy, and so that we get a better understanding of the extent to which policies impact people's lives. Sometimes we miss that connection.

Your lives and all of our lives are powerfully affected by the policies implemented by our government. That's why these stories are so important. These stories help push the country to make the changes that we're going to need to make for military families.

I'm joined here on stage by five military spouses. They each have their own perspectives on the issues that matter most to their lives. Whether it's more efficient VA systems, or TRICARE, or education for their children, or more resources for returning men and women—whatever it may be—they all have a unique perspective.

All of the women up here know that it's tough to make the balance—to balance career and raising children while their spouses are away. They are united in a vision we all share, of a system that does more to support its military families, both when a spouse is deployed but also long after he or she returns.

Barack and I know that too often it feels like you're alone, on your own, in this struggle. I've heard stories all over this country of military families trying to hold it together with not enough support.

I know that you become everything. You become everything to your family. You are mom *and* dad. You're in charge of the checkbook and handing out discipline, trying to get school supplies and make sure they're ready for the start of the school year.

Many of you are taking care of in-laws and elderly family members while your spouses are away, and trying to make dinner, and trying to get laundry done. And then, as the bills start piling up and the nights seem longer, you have the added responsibility of worrying late into the night about how you're going to manage it with not enough earnings coming in.

If there's one thing I've learned at these roundtables, it's that when our military goes to war, their families go with them. We have to remember that.

And I know that many of these marriages face unique challenges. I've heard people talk about the fact that when their spouse may be deployed for months at a time, in the toughest conditions imaginable, and then they come home with problems that spouses simply aren't equipped to deal with. There can be a stigma attached with trying to get help.

Or, they come home and life is good, but there is a significant re-adjustment period, and as soon as things start getting back to normal, they're re-deployed. They go right back out. The bags are packed, and they start *all* over again.

What has also struck me in talking to these military spouses is just how much they take care of each other. Barack and I see how the military is really like a family.

And it has to be. You fill in when the services fail, as they often do. From babysitting to untangling the bureaucracy, to delivering bad news—even if people aren't trained to do it all, they do it anyway, because they have to.

I'll never forget a moment on a panel when a young mother stood up. She was in tears. She talked about how she felt alone, how she didn't know how to handle it with a young child and a limited education, even though she was trying to get her education. One woman stood up and said, 'I don't know you. I've never met you before but I will give you my number, my email address. You will no longer be alone because I am here.'

All the other women on that panel stood up right along with that young woman. It was a... it was a hopeful experience.

That's the kind of courage and strength military spouses show us every single day, in the shadows. And we don't even know it.

They're doing everything that's asked of them and more. And they're not asking for much. They're not asking for anyone to feel sorry for them. They're proud of what they are doing. They are not asking government to solve all their problems. Not at all. Not for one second.

They're just asking for a Washington that understands and recognizes the challenges that military families face as part of their extraordinary commitment to our country.

Let me tell you something, my husband, Barack Obama understands that commitment. And he believes in the commitment that America *must* make to its military families.

Barack's grandfather enlisted after Pearl Harbor. He marched in Patton's Army. And Barack's grandmother worked on a bomber assembly line while her husband was gone. Barack's mother was born at Fort Leavenworth.

His grandfather returned to a country that gave him the opportunity to go to college on the G.I. Bill, to buy their first home with a loan from the Federal Housing Administration, and move his family west—all the way to Hawaii where he and Barack's grandmother helped to raise him.

So Barack, because of this story and experience, is determined to see that America makes the same commitment today that it made to his grandfather's generation so many years ago."

Akron, Ohio

At a campaign rally

October 24, 08

Michelle steps in for Barack while he visits his grandmother in Hawaii—two and a half weeks prior to her death.

"What I've been trying to tell folks—I am doing this because I happen to be married to a man who gets it. Barack Obama gets it. And let me tell you, he doesn't get it in some disconnected philosophical way. He gets it because he's lived it.

See, there's something that happens to folks when they grow up regular. Barack is a product of a whole lot of hard work. There's something that happens to you when your mother was eighteen years old when she had you—a single parent mother—and you see her struggle. You know that she's doing the best that she can. All that she's trying to teach you is when you trip, stumble, maybe when you fall, that you get back up.

There's something that affects the way you see the world and how you think about other people and their lives. You're more empathetic. You're more open. You're more compassionate.

And then there's something that happens to you when you see that same woman lose her life.

At fifty-three (she was a young woman) she died of ovarian cancer. And to watch her at a time, like millions of Americans, when she should have been thinking about her own health, she should have been reflecting on her life because she knew she was going to die. She knew she had stage four cancer.

At a time when she should have been meeting with her family and taking long walks in the park, and just being at peace, she was worrying whether the insurance companies were going to cover her health care cost, because they told her that cancer was a pre-existing condition.

That is happening to millions of Americans across this country..."

Appendix

Inaugural Address

National Mall, Washington D.C.

January 20, 2009

Barack Obama was sworn in as the 44th president of the United States and the nation's first African-American President on Tuesday, Jan 20, 2009.

"Thank you. Thank you.

My fellow citizens:

I stand here today humbled by the task before us, grateful for the trust you have bestowed, mindful of the sacrifices borne by our ancestors. I thank President Bush for his service to our nation, as well as the generosity and cooperation he has shown throughout this transition.

Forty-four Americans have now taken the presidential oath. The words have been spoken during rising tides of prosperity and the still waters of peace. Yet, every so often, the oath is taken amidst gathering clouds and raging storms. At these moments, America has carried on not simply because of the skill or vision of those in high office, but because We the People have remained faithful to the ideals of our fore bearers and true to our founding documents.

So it has been. So it must be with this generation of Americans.

That we are in the midst of crisis is now well understood. Our nation is at war against a far-reaching network of violence and hatred. Our economy is badly weakened, a consequence of greed and irresponsibility on the part of some, but also our collective failure to make hard choices and prepare the nation for a new age. Homes have been lost; jobs shed; businesses shuttered. Our health care is too costly; our schools fail too many; and each day brings further evidence that the ways we use energy strengthen our adversaries and threaten our planet.

These are the indicators of crisis, subject to data and statistics. Less measurable but no less profound is a sapping of confidence across our land, a nagging fear that America's decline is inevitable, that the next generation must lower its sights.

Today I say to you that the challenges we face are real. They are serious and they are many. They will not be met easily or in a short span of time. But know this, America: They *will* be met.

On this day, we gather because we have chosen hope over fear, unity of purpose over conflict and discord. On this day, we come to proclaim an end to the petty grievances and false promises, the recriminations and worn-out dogmas, that for far too long have strangled our politics.

We remain a young nation, but in the words of Scripture, the time has come to set aside childish things. The time has come to reaffirm our enduring spirit, to choose our better history, to carry forward that precious gift, that noble idea, passed on from generation to generation: the God-given promise that all are equal, all are free, and all deserve a chance to pursue their full measure of happiness.

In reaffirming the greatness of our nation, we understand that greatness is never a given. It must be earned. Our journey has never been one of shortcuts or settling for less. It has not been the path for the fainthearted—for those who prefer leisure over work, or seek only the pleasures of riches and fame.

Rather, it has been the risk-takers, the doers, the makers of things—some celebrated but more often, men and women obscure in their labor—who have carried us up the long, rugged path toward prosperity and freedom.

For us, they packed up their few worldly possessions and traveled across oceans in search of a new life.

For us, they toiled in sweatshops and settled the West, endured the lash of the whip and plowed the hard earth.

For us, they fought and died, in places like Concord and Gettysburg, Normandy and Khe Sahn.

Time and again, these men and women struggled and sacrificed and worked till their hands were raw so that we might live a better life. They saw America as bigger than the sum of our individual ambitions, greater than all the differences of birth or wealth or faction.

This is the journey we continue today.

We remain the most prosperous, powerful nation on Earth. Our workers are no less productive than when this crisis began. Our minds are no less inventive, our goods and services no less needed than they were last week or last month or last year.

Our capacity remains undiminished. But our time of standing pat, of protecting narrow interests and putting off unpleasant decisions—that time has surely passed. Starting today, we must pick ourselves up, dust ourselves off, and begin again the work of remaking America.

For everywhere we look, there is work to be done. The state of the economy calls for action, bold and swift, and we will act—not only to create new jobs, but to lay a new foundation for growth. We will build the roads and bridges, the electric grids and digital lines that feed our commerce and bind us together. We will restore science to its rightful place, and wield technology's wonders to raise health care's quality and lower its cost. We will harness the sun and the winds and the soil to fuel our cars and run our factories. And we will transform our schools and colleges and universities to meet the demands of a new age. All this we *can* do. And all this we *will* do.

Now, there are some who question the scale of our ambitions—who suggest that our system cannot tolerate too many big plans. Their memories are short. For they have forgotten what this country has already done, what free men and women can achieve when imagination is joined to common purpose, and necessity to courage.

What the cynics fail to understand is that the ground has shifted beneath them, that the stale political arguments that have consumed us for so long no longer apply.

The question we ask today is not whether our government is too big or too small, but whether it works—whether it helps families find jobs at a decent wage, care they can afford, a retirement that is dignified. Where the answer is yes, we intend to move forward. Where the answer is no, programs will end. And those of us who manage the public's dollars will be held to account to spend wisely, reform bad habits, and do our business in the light of day—because only then can we restore the vital trust between a people and their government.

Nor is the question before us whether the market is a force for good or ill. Its power to generate wealth and expand freedom is unmatched, but this crisis has reminded us that without a watchful eye, the market can spin out of control. The nation cannot prosper long when it favors only the prosperous. The success of our economy has always depended not just on the size of our gross domestic product, but on the reach of our prosperity—on the ability to extend opportunity to every willing heart—not out of charity, but because it is the surest route to our common good.

As for our common defense, we reject as false the choice between our safety and our ideals. Our Founding Fathers, faced with perils we can scarcely imagine, drafted a charter to assure the rule of law and the rights of man. A charter expanded by the blood of generations. Those ideals still light the world, and we will not give them up for expedience's sake.

And so to all other peoples and governments who are watching today, from the grandest capitals to the small village where my father was born: know that America is a friend of each nation and every man, woman and child who seeks a future of peace and dignity, and we are ready to lead once more.

Recall that earlier generations faced down fascism and communism not just with missiles and tanks, but with sturdy alliances and enduring convictions. They understood that our power alone cannot protect us, nor does it entitle us to do as we please. Instead, they knew that our power grows through its prudent use. Our security emanates from the justness of our cause, the force of our example, the tempering qualities of humility and restraint.

We are the keepers of this legacy. Guided by these principles once more, we can meet those new threats that demand even greater effort, even greater cooperation and understanding between nations. We will begin to responsibly leave Iraq to its people and forge a hard earned peace in Afghanistan.

With old friends and former foes, we will work tirelessly to lessen the nuclear threat and roll back the specter of a warming planet. We will not apologize for our way of life, nor will we waver in its defense.

And for those who seek to advance their aims by inducing terror and slaughtering innocents, we say to you now that our spirit is stronger and cannot be broken. You cannot outlast us, and we will defeat you.

For we know that our patchwork heritage is a strength, not a weakness. We are a nation of Christians and Muslims, Jews and Hindus, and nonbelievers. We are shaped by every language and culture, drawn from every end of this Earth. And because we have tasted the bitter swill of civil war and segregation, and emerged from that dark chapter stronger and more united, we cannot help but believe that the old hatreds shall someday pass, that the lines of tribe shall soon dissolve, that as the world grows smaller, our common humanity shall reveal itself, and that America must play its role in ushering in a new era of peace.

To the Muslim world: we seek a new way forward, based on mutual interest and mutual respect. To those leaders around the globe who seek to sow conflict, or blame their society's ills on the West: know that your people will judge you on what you can build, not what you destroy. To those who cling to power through corruption and deceit and the silencing of dissent: know that you are on the wrong side of history; but that we will extend a hand if you are willing to unclench your fist.

To the people of poor nations: we pledge to work alongside you to make your farms flourish and let

110

clean waters flow, to nourish starved bodies and feed hungry minds. And to those nations like ours that enjoy relative plenty: we say we can no longer afford indifference to the suffering outside our borders; nor can we consume the world's resources without regard to effect. For the world has changed, and we must change with it.

As we consider the road that unfolds before us, we remember with humble gratitude those brave Americans who, at this very hour, patrol far-off deserts and distant mountains. They have something to tell us, just as the fallen heroes who lie in Arlington whisper through the ages. We honor them not only because they are guardians of our liberty, but because they embody the spirit of service, a willingness to find meaning in something greater than themselves. And yet, at this moment, a moment that will define a generation, it is precisely this spirit that must inhabit us *all*.

For as much as government can do and must do, it is ultimately the faith and determination of the American people upon which this nation relies. It is the kindness to take in a stranger when the levees break, the selflessness of workers who would rather cut their hours than see a friend lose their job which sees us through our darkest hours. It is the firefighter's courage to storm a stairway filled with smoke, but also a parent's willingness to nurture a child, that finally decides our fate.

Our challenges may be new. The instruments with which we meet them may be new. But those values upon which our success depends - honesty and hard work, courage and fair play, tolerance and curiosity, loyalty and patriotism—these things are old. These things are true. They have been the quiet force of progress throughout our history.

What is demanded then, is a return to these truths. What is required of us now, is a new era of responsibility—a recognition on the part of every American that we have duties to ourselves, our nation, and the world. Duties that we do not grudgingly accept but rather seize gladly, firm in the knowledge that there is nothing so satisfying to the spirit, so defining of our character, than giving our all to a difficult task.

This is the price and the promise of citizenship.

This is the source of our confidence—the knowledge that God calls on us to shape an uncertain destiny.

This is the meaning of our liberty and our creed—why men and women and children of every race and every faith can join in celebration across this magnificent Mall, and why a man whose father less than 60 years ago might not have been served at a local restaurant can now stand before you to take a most sacred oath.

So let us mark this day with remembrance, of who we are and how far we have traveled. In the year of America's birth, in the coldest of months, a small band of patriots huddled by dying campfires on the shores of an icy river. The capital was abandoned. The enemy was advancing. The snow was stained with blood. At a moment when the outcome of our revolution was most in doubt, the father of our nation ordered these words be read to the people:

'Let it be told to the future world, that in the depth of winter, when nothing but hope and virtue could survive... that the city and the country, alarmed at one common danger, came forth to meet [it].'

America:

In the face of our common dangers, in this winter of our hardship, let us remember these timeless words. With hope and virtue, let us brave once more the icy currents, and endure what storms may come. Let it be said by our children's children that when we were tested, we refused to let this journey end, that we did not turn back, nor did we falter; and with eyes fixed on the horizon and God's grace upon us, we carried forth that great gift of freedom and delivered it safely to future generations.

Thank you. God bless you.

And God bless the United States of America."

CPSIA information can be obtained at www.ICGtesting.com
Printed in the USA
LVOW081641080313

323402LV00003B/339/P